THE GOD TRANSFORMED LIFE

RELATING WITH GOD THROUGH HIS WORD

by
Esau C. Maponda

THE LIFE OF GOD IN A BELIEVER

Grosvenor House
Publishing Limited

All rights reserved
Copyright © Esau C. Maponda, 2020

The right of Esau C. Maponda to be identified as the author of this
work has been asserted in accordance with Section 78
of the Copyright, Designs and Patents Act 1988

The book cover is copyright to Daniel Cotton - DC Media

This book is published by
Grosvenor House Publishing Ltd
Link House
140 The Broadway, Tolworth, Surrey, KT6 7HT.
www.grosvenorhousepublishing.co.uk

This book is sold subject to the conditions that it shall not, by way of
trade or otherwise, be lent, resold, hired out or otherwise circulated
without the author's or publisher's prior consent in any form of binding or
cover other than that in which it is published and
without a similar condition including this condition being imposed
on the subsequent purchaser.

All rights reserved.
This book may not be copied or reprinted for commercial gain or profit.
The use of short quotations or occassional page copying for personal use
or group study is permitted and encouraged. Permission will be granted
upon request. Unless otherwise identified, scripture quotations are from
the English Standard Version of the Bible.

A CIP record for this book
is available from the British Library

ISBN 978-1-83975-058-8

'Man shall not live on bread alone but by every word that comes
from the mouth of God'
(Matthew 4:4)

DEDICATION

To our God, the same yesterday today and forever – may your word grow mightily and prevail.

To believers – may the quest for the Word of God consume you, as God connects with you intimately through His Word.

CONTENTS

PREFACE VII

INTRODUCTION IX

1. THE PURPOSE OF THE WORD OF GOD 1

2. THE NATURE OF THE WORD OF GOD 11

3. NURTURING THE RELATIONSHIP WITH
   THE WORD OF GOD 17

   A RICH VIEW OF THE WORD OF GOD 18

   RESPONDING TO THE WORD OF GOD 26

   THE VALUE OF THE WORD OF GOD 34

   GOD'S PART OR FACTOR IN RELATING
   WITH HIS WORD 36

   THE IMPACT OF GOD'S WORD IN THE
   BELIEVER'S LIFE 39

4. WORD FITNESS FOR NEW BELIEVERS 41

5. WHAT NEXT? – WORD FITNESS! 45

WORD FITNESS WORKBOOK 49

ACKNOWLEDGMENTS 57

PREFACE

*"... And we also thank God continually for this, that when you received **the word of God** [concerning salvation] which you heard from us, **you welcomed it not as the word of [mere] men, but as it truly is, the word of God**, which is **effectually at work in you who believe** [exercising its inherent, supernatural power in those of faith]."* (1 Thessalonians 2:13 AMP – bold emphasis mine).

Our view and response to the word of God is important in our walk of faith. God is intimately connecting with us through His word. When you engage with the word of God it is not just like human ideas, but it is indeed, the word of God working in our lives to transform us. The quest for such an intimacy with God through His Word has been and is my lifelong pursuit, and God has deposited some truths in my life that I cannot hold back but share!

May God stimulate in you that passion to connect with Him through His word in faith and trust, as we eagerly wait for the coming back of our Lord Jesus Christ.

INTRODUCTION

A Quest for Truth…

My life was transformed in 2001 when Ecclesiastes 1:2 became alive in my heart. "Vanity of vanities," says the preacher, "vanity of vanities! All is vanity" (Ecclesiastes 1:2). That marked the turning point for my life; weighing the value of all my pursuits, and that of a fulfilling relationship with God. I chose the pursuit of knowing God and that remains incomparable to all available options.

Reflecting on my Christian walk, the greatest influence in my life comes from a deep passion for the Word of God. One of my early bibles was the *NIV Quest Study Bible*, which I took to be a 'quest for the truth' and that is what God deposited in me. I recall how at University my friends and I were so passionate about the word of God and about the truth; imitating the Bereans in the book of Acts 17:11, who after hearing the apostles would confirm what they heard by referring to the scriptures. We went to such an extent of searching the scriptures in the middle of a sermon (a bit extreme) but such was our passion for the truth.

The primary anchor of my relationship with God is my engagement with His Word in its various forms. My prayer for you, as you read this book, is that the Lord may give to you a passion for His Word. Indeed, we cannot live by bread alone but by every word that comes from God (Matthew 4:4).

In the last few years, meditating on Psalm 119 has blessed my heart as the psalm gives such a rich view of the Word of God that if grasped, transforms lives. My desire is that it changes yours, just as it does mine.

Who else other than David, a man after God's heart (1 Samuel 13:14; Acts 13:22) can articulate the manifold nature of the Word of God? In this book, I share reflections from this Psalm and what God helped me grasp.

My heart's desire is that you reflect on the importance of the Word of God in your life and yield yourself to its power to transform you so that you can experience the fullness of God's Kingdom life. God is intimately connecting with us through his word.

1.

THE PURPOSE OF THE WORD OF GOD

Metamorphosis...

<u>Do I know myself?</u>

As a new Christian, there were intriguing truths that left indelible impressions in my heart. I attended college at the National University of Science and Technology (NUST) in Zimbabwe and there I joined the Christian Union group. I was in the company of brothers and sisters who were passionate about God. They taught us about the new creation realities, how when we made that important decision to accept Christ, we became new creations and how the old self had passed away entering new realities (2 Corinthians 5:17). Around the same time, I took to study Watchmen Nee's teachings on the spirit, soul and body, from his book *The Spiritual Man*. The study unlocked an amazing perspective of the believer's anatomy. Trying to reconcile the picture painted by the scriptures and my present personal views, left me with a quest to find out more. Paul spoke of being sanctified wholly spirit, soul, and body (1 Thessalonians 5:23) that challenged me to ask God for answers.

As I grew in my appreciation of my make up, I realised that this is not apparent in my daily living and my passion was to find a way to uncover the treasure in me (2 Corinthians 4:7).

The writer of Hebrews gave me some insights, the Word of God is sharper than any double-edged sword to the separation of the soul and the spirit and bone and marrow and nothing is hidden from the word of God (Hebrews 4:12). This was a eureka moment of understanding how to reconcile the picture painted by the scriptures and the believers' transformation; the Word of God has the ability to help me distinguish between my soul and my spirit. We often neglect the spirit man (inner man) as he is not apparent to our natural senses but is made clear to us by God's revelation. When we stand in front of the natural mirror, what we see is the mass of our bodies, hence we make more effort in looking after that which we can see, touch and smell. James brings to our attention the spiritual mirror which helps us have the correct view of the inner man, in James 1:22–26 he gives a similitude of how looking into the natural mirror is like looking into the perfect law of liberty (Word of God). If you really want to see what and how you look like in the inner man look at the mirror, the Word of God.

You can have a changed life!

This was important to me because John noted that the time was coming when true worshippers would worship God in spirit and in truth (John 4:24). How can I do that if I am not able to tap into my spirit man and transfer the riches, he possesses into my whole being that is soul and body? Brother Paul highlighted; who knows a man than his spirit and who knows God than His Spirit and the man's spirit commune with God's Spirit in a way that changes lives (1 Corinthians 2:6–16). The quest in my heart intensified, in search for that window into this glorious life and Kingdom of God.

The drive was and is that, my salvation was not just for statistics in the Kingdom of God; not to be like one of the Old Testament folk described as having had a family and children and lived a certain number of years and died, but rather be like Jabez, he caused the writer's pattern of writing to change (1 Chronicles 4:9). Paul puts it in a simple way, getting hold of the reason God saved me (Philippians 3:12–14).

Now Paul in Romans 12:1-2 says something significant. After having explained the mercies of God, what Christ has done leading to our salvation, he then speaks of our transformation by the renewing of our minds. The original Greek word used for the transformation is the same that applies to the change from a caterpillar to a butterfly. Simply put he is saying my brothers and sisters; we have the potential to have changed lives equivalent to that of changing from a caterpillar to a butterfly, what a word!

Metamorphosis

In a past visit to Malaga in Spain, one of my memorable and exciting moments was a visit to a Butterfly park in Benalmadena. After enjoying all the butterfly watching and photo capturing the most intriguing part of the visit was reflecting on the butterfly's formative process (metamorphosis). This is the process of changing from an immature form to an adult form in two or more distinct stages. For the butterfly, its transformation is from the caterpillar to the pupa then from pupa to the adult butterfly. This is amazing, a miracle at best. I observed from this process that a caterpillar and a butterfly are two different creatures, the butterfly will still live in the same world with the caterpillar, but a vast difference is now noticeable. The time spent in the cocoon is when the change happens; the caterpillar needs to have eaten a lot when it goes through the change process.

The key message from Paul's discourse is transformation through the renewing of our minds; bringing the question of how then do we do that? He explains this in Ephesians 4:17–31 when he talks about walking in the newness of life; he outlines what this transformation looks like. In this passage, he highlights three crucial requirements for the believer, which are to <u>put off your old self, renewal in the spirit of your minds,</u> and to <u>put on the new self</u> – created in Christ Jesus. In between the putting off and putting on there is the renewing of the spirit of our minds. The transformation is putting off the old manner of life and putting on the new manner of life (self), created after the likeness of God in true righteousness.

<u>*The Word of God has the power to change lives*</u>

The thought of a renewed mind, is exciting, but what is the key to the process? In Ephesians, Paul talks of the great mystery between the church and himself, in it he unpacks the secret for a renewed mind.

> *"...that he might sanctify her, having cleansed her by the washing of water with the word, so that he might present the church to himself in splendour, without spot or wrinkle or any such thing, that she might be holy and without blemish"*. (Ephesians 5:26–27).

The Word of God has a cleansing and sanctifying ability. Jesus says sanctify them by your truth and your word is the truth (John 17:17). The word of God is the objective truth; the only thing that can change the realities of our lives is the entrance of the truth.

When we become aware of the new creation realities the more we can put on the new self and put off the old manner of life. David puts it as the entrance of God's word makes wise the simple (Psalm 119:130) and Jesus says you shall know the truth and the truth shall make you free and his word is truth (John 8:32; John 17:17). Anytime the world does not accept the Word of God it is robbed of the truth that if accepted will change their lives. The truth that you possess allows you to identify what to put off and what to put on. Jesus said something so remarkable in His priestly prayer: "And this is eternal life, that they know you the only true God, and Jesus Christ whom you have sent" (John 17:3). The Word therefore allows us to know more of God and so we can put on more of the true reflection of Him. Therefore, the transformation of our lives as believers' hinges on our relationship (regard and conduct towards) with the Word of God. The primary purpose of the word of God is to transform (metamorphosis) our lives.

Therefore, if the primary purpose of the Word of God is transformation in the believer's life then our relationship with the Word is of paramount importance. How we respond to and regard the Word of God determines the levels of transformation we experience. I spoke of how the caterpillar changes to a butterfly and how we can change from our old manner of life (self) to the new manner of life (self) and the need to manifest that new manner of life (self). How the caterpillar changes to a butterfly is a mystery to some, but we know it is the work of God, likewise it is the work of God by His Word and Spirit that the believer's human life is transformed. As Paul helped us to understand the need for the renewal of the spirit of our minds, I caught the glimpse of how that works, and the key elements involved.

The parable of the sower in Matthew 13:18–23 brings to life the key elements of the effective working of the Word; the seed is the Word of God; the ground is the human heart and its response to the Word and linking the fruit to the ground's (heart's) response to the Word of God. The Word must be heard, must be responded to and depending on the response then fruit yield is in varying degrees of hundred, sixty and thirty percent. In another parable in Mark 4:26–29, if the sower does his job and the ground is good, there is increase in varying degrees. We may not understand how it comes about but we know it does. Paul in 1 Corinthians 3:5–7 highlights the planting and watering process, but the ultimate truth is that only God gives growth or increase.

Therefore, effectively by having the Word in our hearts, regarding it highly and responding positively creates capacity in us for God to give growth. The seed of the Word begins to renew the spirit of our minds and the manifestation of him who is in the image of God (i.e. the spirit man) the new creature begins to show in our lives. The Word of God is the source of the transformation but with responsibilities on the believer and God. This transformation of a believer is not a one-off event, but a lifetime process as illustrated in the next section.

The believer's daily transformation cycle

Every day brings an opportunity to see God change our lives (views, attitudes, priorities, values, aspirations, and destiny) within our context. It starts with the sowing of the word of God into our lives (exposing ourselves directly or indirectly to His word) and responding to the truth brought to our attention, secondly God is the one who uses that word to work inside of us to be willing and to take pleasure in acting on the word (Phil 2:13). Thirdly as we realise and become more aware of the truth, we start to leave our old manner of life and embracing the new life in God (having a biblical perspective to life). Finally, as we yield more and more to the dictates of the word of God and the Holy Spirit, our lives become fruitful in every aspect in varying levels (there is no one measure of success for every believer, but God gives success in line with His ultimate purposes). Ultimately you begin to live life with a purpose and meaning beyond societal standards and measures. An example is someone who used to earn a living through stealing and when they receive the Lord Jesus Christ as their personal saviour, they are exposed to the truth that God is our Shepherd and meets our needs through Jesus (Psalm 23; John 10). They are encouraged to work with their hands and to steal no more, they will begin to understand why the command to not steal was put by God. By stealing they are publicly expressing that God is not able to provide for them, which is contrary to their intended expression of the life of Christ in them. What should they do? the bible says God blesses the work of our hands (Deuteronomy 28:12), they will start to look for work to do to have a means of living. The more this goes on, God will bless them and increase the rewards from their work because God is faithful to His word. Do you see that, it is a daily process which we should intentionally and patiently engage in.

Man shall not live by bread alone, but by every word that comes from the mouth of God (Matthew 4:4). The way we cannot go without food should apply when it comes to the Word of God in the believer's life.

THE GOD TRANSFORMED LIFE

What does a transformed life look like?

Transformation must be intentional, and a priority reflected in the way we regard and respond to the Word of God. When it comes to the Word taking root in my heart in order to produce fruit there is the God factor, the Word factor and the believer (individual) factor (condition and response of the believer's heart).

It is a necessity to paint the picture of the end game; otherwise, it will be difficult to measure progress. What does the transformation that emanates from the Word of God look like? We must look at the end-to-end process and not start and stop at salvation. The original intent of God for man is that man be in the image and likeness of Himself (God). Paul speaking in Ephesians points to the truth that we need to grow to the full stature of Christ (Ephesians 4:13), for who else other than Christ is the full expression of God.

I view the transformation that engaging with the Word of God brings at three levels:

1. Exhibiting the character of God – fruit of the Spirit (Galatians 5:22–23).
2. Walking in the fullness of the Spirit of God (Isaiah 11:1–2, Ephesians 3:19).
3. Becoming a practitioner of the word of God – Doers of the Word, full of life-giving works of faith (James 1:22–26).

Paul in his writings to the Corinthian believers makes it appear as though it is a foregone conclusion that every believer should understand that they are the temple of the living God and that the Spirit of God resides in them (1 Corinthians 6:19, 2 Corinthians 6:16). The Holy Spirit uses the Word of God to transform our lives, Paul comments on this while writing to the Ephesian believers when he says, "… and the Sword of the Spirit which is the Word of God" (Ephesians 6:17).

Transformation leads therefore to a deep communion with the Holy Spirit and that translates into us exhibiting the character of God through the fruit of the Spirit. Our approach to believers, non-believers, work, circumstances and all other areas of life will be with love, joy, peace, patience, kindness, goodness, faithfulness, gentleness, and self-control (Galatians 5:22–23).

Secondly, we will allow the full operation of the Holy Spirit in our lives as the Spirit of the Lord, Spirit of wisdom and understanding, the Spirit of counsel and might, and the Spirit of knowledge and the fear of God (Isaiah 11:2).

Thirdly, our desire becomes that of being doers of the word of God, we show our obedience to the Lordship of the Word by doing the Word; becoming open letters of God to the world by our manner of life (2 Corinthians 3:2). That is exhibiting transformation from the Word of God. It is evident that you cannot separate the work of God the Father, the Holy Spirit and Jesus from their Word; as the scriptures are clear on this that in the beginning was the Word, the Word was with God, and the Word was God (John 1:1).

2.

THE NATURE OF THE WORD OF GOD

The words I have spoken to you are spirit and life…

> *"Long ago, at many times and in many ways, God spoke to our fathers by the prophets, but in these last days he has spoken to us by his Son, whom he appointed the heir of all things, through whom also he created the world. He is the radiance of the glory of God and the exact imprint of his nature, and he upholds the universe by the word of his power"* (Hebrews 1:1–3).

There is a higher call in our generation to understand how God is speaking to us today, as that establishes a foundation of how we seek his voice and responses. We may not have lived at the time when God spoke out of the mountain to Moses and Abraham and through individual prophets. We are past the time when Christ the Word was made flesh (John 1:14) and walked the earth expressing God in words, actions, thoughts and life, but we need to have a proper view of how then we can relate with Him. We now have the declared word, which are the scriptures (The Bible) at our disposal to relate with Christ as John explained:

"That which was from the beginning, which we have heard, which we have seen with our eyes, which we have looked upon, and our hands have handled, concerning the Word of life the life was manifested, and we have seen, and bear witness, and declare to you that eternal life which was with the Father and was manifested to us that which we have seen and heard we declare to you, that you also may have fellowship with us; and truly our fellowship is with the Father and with His Son Jesus Christ. And these things we write to you that your joy may be full" (1 John 1:1–4 NKJV).

Brothers and sisters if we do not have the proper view of the scriptures, we can miss the fellowship, the intended purpose of John's message. Years back when Jesus was here on earth, he gave an insightful rebuke, they were busy searching the writings (scripture) and missing the person, referenced by the scriptures.

But you do not have His word abiding in you, because whom He sent, Him you do not believe. You search the Scriptures, for in them you think you have eternal life; and these are they which testify of me. However, you are not willing to come to me that you may have life (John 5: 38–40 NKJV).

We run the risk of just seeing the writings in the Bible and not seeing their purpose, they are the channel for us to relate with the person of Christ. The Word of God is more than just the writings we see in the Bible, but access into the thoughts and mind of God. When you read the scriptures, you need to have the correct view that you are interacting with Divinity, with a person and these are not mere writings.

When you spend time in the scriptures, you are getting an insight into the character, nature and being of God. You come face to face with real people, with real life issues and having the real God.

It is the spirit who gives life; the flesh is no help at all: the words that I have spoken to you, are spirit and life (John 6:63).

The black and white writing is not the one that gives life, but the message of God carried in the black and white writing. The writings are like a packaging of the message; the message is the one, which is *spirit and life in nature*. The more you engage with the book (The Bible) the more you engage with the life of God and it is spiritual not fleshly. The words of God are carriers of His life and His Spirit, the more intake we have the more he quickens our lives. The writer of the book of Hebrews, informs us that the Word of God is sharper than any double-edged sword to the separation of the soul and the spirit, bone and marrow and nothing is hidden from Him (Hebrews 4:12). All else that speaks to our lives must be weighed and measured from the perspective of the full revealed Word of God in the Bible, which shall not be added to.

Having grown up in an agrarian society, I understand the power of a seed. The nature and type of harvest is dependent on the type of seed and the preparations of the fields. The *nature of the Word of God is that of a seed* and not only that, but, an incorruptible seed.

Having been born again, not of corruptible seed, but of incorruptible, through the word of God, which lives and abides forever (1 Peter 1:23).

This understanding is crucial for believers, we realise that we have a responsibility in determining the harvests we receive in the Kingdom of God.

The fields are our hearts, the preparation being how we respond to the Word of God (Luke 8:4–15). Understanding how seeds function makes us dependent on God, as all we can do is receive the seed and prepare our hearts, but God gives the increase.

I did an exercise to explore the manifold nature of the seed (Word of God) in the believers' life, by going through the New Testament references to the Word of God's effects outlined below.

> John 6:68… the **words** of eternal life…
> Acts 5:20… the **words** of this life…
> Acts 13:26… the **word** of this salvation…
> Acts 14:3… the **word** of his grace…
> Acts 20:32… the **word** of his grace…
> Acts 26:25… the **words** of truth and soberness
> Romans 10:8… the **word** of faith…
> 1 Corinthians 12:8… the **word** of wisdom… the **word** of knowledge
> 2 Corinthians 5:19… the **word** of reconciliation…
> 2 Corinthians 6:7… the **word** of truth…
> Ephesians 1:13… the **word** of truth…
> Philippians 2:16… the **word** of life…
> Colossians 1:5… the **word** of the truth…
> 1 Timothy 4:6… the **words** of faith…
> 2 Timothy 2:15… the **word** of truth…
> Hebrews 1:3… the **word** of his power…
> Hebrews 5:13… the **word** of righteousness…

Hebrews 7:28… the **word of** <u>the oath</u>…
James 1:18… the **word of** <u>truth</u>…
2 Peter 1:19… **word of** <u>prophecy</u>…
1 John 1:1… the **Word of** <u>life</u>…
Revelation 1:3… **words of** <u>this prophecy</u>…

Growing up I had a lot of restlessness due to a lot of deep questions that I had about life, purpose and meaning, chaos in the world, suffering to name a few. However, the above exercise effectively showed me that the word of God addresses the deep issues of life, if I give it the attention, humility and trust it deserves. The amazing part is the realisation that the answers or solutions are in fact a person (Jesus Christ), that changes things as the way to know a person is to fellowship more with Him. Look and think deeply on the exercise, the references to the word of God touch on the very essence of our questions in life; eternal life, salvation, grace of God, truth and sober approach to life, faith, wisdom and knowledge, reconciliation to God, power, right standing with God, and our future or tomorrow!

It taught me that whatever I need in life there is a seed for it in the Word of God and I need to consume it more and believe in God for the results.

We have a dual responsibility then of receiving the seed and sowing the seed into the lives of others and circumstances of life through our words, full of the spirit and life of the word of God. In our time and generation, we must engage with the Bible with the understanding that it is not just a book, but we are engaging with the Person of God, the message is not in human nature, but it is spirit and produces life. The message of the scriptures becomes seed for us to receive, which imparts the fullness of God in our lives and we need to sow the same seed into other people's (believers and non-believers) lives and every circumstance in life through our words, actions and thoughts.

3.

NURTURING THE RELATIONSHIP WITH THE WORD OF GOD

The sum of your word is truth...

Who else other than David, a man after God's heart (I Sam. 13:14; Acts 13:22) can articulate the manifold nature of the Word of God and how we are supposed to regard and respond to the Word of God in such a marvellous relationship? In a recent study, I took some time to go through Psalm 119 and the nuggets I got from my meditations were amazing. This expanded my view of the Word of God and my expected response when relating with the Word. In this chapter, I discuss my observations from five perspectives:

(a) David's view of the Word of God.
(b) David's response to the Word of God.
(c) The value of the Word of God to David.
(d) God's part or factor in relation to His Word.
(e) The impact of God's Word on David's life.

A RICH VIEW OF THE WORD OF GOD

David refers to the Word of God using various terms to reveal his view of the Word of God, showing its intended effect and potency in his life. In Psalm 119; he refers to the Word of God as; the **Law** of the Lord, His **Testimonies**, His **Judgements**, His **Precepts**, His **Ordinances**, **Truth**, **Words**, His **Ways**, **Commandments**, **Statutes** and His **Justice**.

David ruled over a kingdom and for us to appreciate these references we need to understand that we are in the Kingdom of God; following our translation from the kingdom of darkness into the Kingdom of Light (Colossians 1:13).

We have God as our King and the unique part of our kingdom is that we are kings too and He is the King of kings. We have God as the ultimate authority. Trying to define these terms from a dictionary perspective limits our understanding and comprehension, the effort here then is to help trigger thoughts that only God can then give a full expression in our hearts. I will deal with these references in the context of the Kingdom of God to provide the essence of David's revelation of the Word of God (Matthew 6:10).

David refers to the Word of God as the Truth

This is such a deep understanding. Jesus said to Pilate, "for this purpose, I was born and for this purpose I have come into the world to bear witness to the truth and everyone who is of the truth listens to my voice," and Pilate had to ask, "what is truth?" (John 18:37–38). This remains a pertinent question in today's world as the world has taken the truth to be relative or circumstantial. In this age there appears to be no one source of truth where 'truth' is hinged on men esteeming their own knowledge of what is right and wrong based on their minds, desires and pursuits (Genesis 3:5–7). In the Old Testament, God declares that He is not a man that He should lie or the son of man that he should repent (Numbers 23:19). So out of the mouth of God comes only the truth, which is not subject to lies or changes. Jesus is The Way, The Truth and The Life. He is not 'a' truth but 'The' Truth (John 14:6). David appreciates that when he interacts with the Word of God, he is interacting with *reality that is not subject to change (the truth)*.

The truth is not subject to culture, geography, race, generation or circumstances, but transcends all and remains constant and consistent. Oh my God! What a revelation that David had, walking in the word of God is walking in the reality of life, which is objective and not relative.

He understood that living by His Word was not a trial and error approach to life, guesswork or another way of finding positive self-improvement, but rather the experiencing of reality. Paul says: "For the message of the cross is foolishness to those that are perishing, but to us who are being saved it is the power of God," (1 Corinthians 1:18), the truth in its simplicity is bound to be ridiculed, but when one understands that the Word of God is the truth, that is the beginning of a full life. Sin remains sin in God's eyes regardless of how acceptable it may be in a society and in the same vein, if God says you are a new creation that is the reality regardless of your feelings or thoughts. The important thing becomes to fill yourself with the truth of new creation realities, just as David understood and did.

*David refers to the Word of God as His **Word***

David's reference to the Word of God as His word is particularly important as it enables us to realise that whether spoken or written it is the expression of God. Unless He expresses His thoughts and being, we would not be able to know Him. Our God is knowable, as He expresses Himself through His Word. The revelation of God is manifold, through creation, His Word and other various modes. I believe David had the comfort that His God is expressive and relational.

Any time we engage the Word of God, we need to know that we are receiving the expression and thoughts of God. It is more than just the writing in the Bible or on a scroll but an exploration into the mind of God.

No wonder it becomes apparent that we cannot live by earthly food alone, but by the expression of God in our lives (Matthew 4:4). I can imagine David conquering many nations and destroying their gods and seeing how they were not relational or expressive to their people and He would boldly declare that His God is the Lord. God makes Himself known, in Psalms God alludes to the fact that he has exalted His Word above His name (Psalm 138:2 MEV). The measure of the integrity of His Word is amazing. In Hebrews, it is worth noting the phrase: "He holds everything together by what He says – powerful words!" His Word is the expression of His power (Hebrews 1:4 MSG).

The disciples' response when Jesus asked them whether they were going to leave Him like the rest of people is very instructive, they responded, "to whom shall we go? You have the words of eternal life" (John 6:68). How wonderful it was for David, engaging with the Word of God, realising it was not a fruitless labour but experiencing the expression and life of God.His Word is alive and active, He expresses Himself daily, the question becomes whether we relate with the Word with this attitude of a relational God expressing Himself to us at our different levels of faith.

*David references the word of God as His **testimonies***

The level of trust accorded to things and people is often a function of their previous accomplishments or reputation; that is the individual's testimonies. When David was about to face Goliath, he recounts of his testimonies, how he had killed his bears and lions, and to him they were incomparable to the uncircumcised philistine (I Samuel 17:36).

When you consider God's record of accomplishments, how can you not trust or believe in Him, who has such an awesome record of accomplishments? It reminds me of Job and his friends, in the book of Job, after 37 Chapters of complaints and human wisdom God breaks His silence and questions Job about His accomplishments. Questioning him about creation, foundations and measurements of the earth, to a point where he says he had spoken without knowledge (Job 38–41).

There is no God like our God, the inhabitants of Canaan melted when they heard of the Israelites and how their God had dried the River Jordan such that the Israelites were walking on dry ground (Joshua 5:1), even Moses composed a song of how God had destroyed the Egyptians when he parted the Red sea (Exodus 15). Babylonian Kings would acknowledge to Daniel that there is no God like Daniel's God after they had seen his God in action, the mouths of lions shut such that they did not devour Daniel (Daniel 6:25–27). If I can trust to sit on a chair without thinking or taking precaution, what about trusting our great God with all that pertains to our lives as He has such an impeccable record behind Him.

This is the view that David approached the word of God with, feeding himself with the works and accomplishments of God and leaving with faith to accomplish great things so that even the faith 'hall of fame' records David as follows:

"And what more shall I say? for time would fail me to tell of Gideon, Barak, Samson, Jephthah, of David and Samuel and the prophets – who through faith conquered kingdoms, enforced justice, obtained promises, stopped the mouths of lions, quenched the power of fire, escaped the edge of the sword, were made strong out of weakness, became mighty in war, put foreign armies to flight."
(Hebrews 11:33–35)

Imagine those moments when you feel like you are in a storm and then you hear or read that your God walked on water and commanded the storms to subside and they obeyed (Matthew 14:22–31). It could be you are in a battle at work or other place and then you hear or read that your God was the fourth man in the fire, in which Shadrach, Meshach, and Abednego were thrown into but not burnt (Daniel 3–4). It is in moments like these, when you understand; indeed, faith comes by hearing and hearing by the Word of God (Romans 10:17). Paul said that writings of the Old Testament were for us as examples of what God can do in our lives (1 Corinthians 10:11). I believe the more David spent time in the word the more he expanded his view of God. He was in a way creating capacity in himself to believe more, as Daniel alludes: "But the people who know their God shall be strong and carry out great exploits". (Daniel 11:32 NKJV)

*David refers to the word of God as His **Ways***

When David refers to the Word of God as His ways, he opens two perspectives that people can have of God when he says the children of Israel knew the acts of God, but Moses knew the *ways* of God (Psalm 103:7). The children of Israel were known for complaining, murmuring and for their stubborn hearts. Wanting to go back to Egypt where they got food and water under slavery, and not willing to bear the faith and patience necessary for them to inherit the promises of God, craving and settling for the temporary pleasures of bondage than pursuing lasting victory. This shows that only knowing God's acts provides a limited perspective resulting in their negative attitude. Moses had the privilege of being in the presence of God (Exodus 33:23) resulting in his different yet deeper perspective of God.

God's approach to problem solving is so different to ours and unless we have a view of how He approaches issues then we will be limited in our walk with Him. There is a way to a miracle and there is the act of a miracle, understanding the difference leads to an empowered life. Recall Jesus when He says to the crowd in John 6:26 you are following me because of the bread that you have eaten. Only following for bread reveals an attitude inclined towards personal satisfaction rather than seeking the Kingdom of God and His righteousness.

The book of Proverbs informs; there is a way that seems right to a man and often leads to destruction, Isaiah expands that by saying His ways are above our ways and His thoughts above our thoughts (Isaiah 55:8–9). David had this understanding that engaging with the Word of God grants access to the view of the ways of God and unlike the Israelites, you then do not limit God in His operation. An understanding of the ways of God entails a continuous victorious life instead of momentary victories kind of life.

*David refers to the word of God as the **law, statutes, ordinances, judgements, precepts** and **justice** of the Lord*

Though we are in this world, we are not of this world Jesus asserts, and in the face of Pilate He echoed these same words, when he indicated that His kingdom was not of this world (John 18:36). We are here as ambassadors of the heavenly kingdom. Jesus taught his disciples to pray asking for the kingdom of God to come and His will be done on earth as it is in heaven (Matthew 6:10).

David himself being a king understood the dynamics of how a kingdom operates. *In light of this, he refers to the word of God as the law, statutes, ordinances, judgements, precepts and justice of the Lord.* In a kingdom, actions and inactions have consequences both positive and negative. It is important to note Paul's instructive words that the law is spiritual (Romans 7:14), if we view the law as mere do's and don'ts or a written code, we do it at our own disadvantage.

God's Kingdom is a spiritual Kingdom hence these are the governing principles of how the Kingdom of God operates. Their purpose is to protect and safeguard the citizens; hence, as we navigate the spiritual realm, we need the guide on how to conduct ourselves in the Kingdom of God.

A kingdom and a democracy are different. In a democracy it's a function of the majority sentiment but in a kingdom, it is the rule of the king that prevails. David understood that for him to be a good ambassador he needed to engage with God's Word so he would have the whole counsel of the governance of heaven by hearing and understanding God's laws, statutes, ordinances, judgements, precepts and justice.

A comprehensive knowledge of these enables us to appropriate the full benefits of our heavenly Kingdom as its bona fide citizens. As we recognise that the law is spiritual and we have a spiritual kingdom, and the more we fellowship with the word of God the more we create capacity to apply the laws, statutes, ordinances, judgements, precepts and justice in order to manifest and experience the Kingdom of God here on earth.

A rich view of the Word of God

David's view of the Word of God was so rich and manifold, able to govern and regulate his approach and conduct to life in a holistic manner.

It becomes apparent then that we should pray for such a perspective and allow God to speak and relate with us without hindrances.

In light of such a great perspective that David reveals of the Word of God, it is clear that we cannot live by bread alone, but by every word that comes from the mouth of God, and we should crave for His Word as new born babies do (Matthew 4:4; 1 Peter 2:2). The richer our view of the Word of God becomes, the greater the capacity we create in our hearts to believe God and walk by faith and not by sight (2 Corinthians 5:7).

RESPONDING TO THE WORD OF GOD

It is easy to enjoy intellectual exchanges of the Word of God with friends and fellow believers and end there, without allowing the word to become part of our beings and life. When the Word becomes flesh, we can see the truth and grace of God manifest through our lives (John 1:14). Practical application of the Word, in our relationships, work, families, and private lives should be the ultimate desire of every believer. How then do we make it part of our lives, inseparable from our verbal and non-verbal conduct? One can read many books and afterward remain with excitement about the knowledge gained and yet the knowledge does not result in change. Not so with David as he read and heard the Word. It is such an honour to see how David responded to the word of God and the resulting effect the word had on him. Just like food, you do not eat for or on behalf of the next person, so it is with the Word of God. We consume it for ourselves and people around us benefit from the overflow of our spiritual wellbeing.

What is the point of reading, hearing and having fellowship with the Word and yet doing nothing about it? Jesus gave a comparison of the responses of people to the Word of God. If its heard and nothing done then it's like building a house on a foundation of sand which will be destroyed by the elements of weather, on the contrary he who hears and responds by doing the word is like one who builds a house on a solid foundation of a rock, which withstands elements of weather (Matthew 7:24–27). Why hear it, when you do not intend to put it into practice? You are merely building on sand and the elements of life will surely knock you down, but if you practice what you hear then you will be able to withstand the elements of life as your foundation is on the rock of ages (Jesus Christ).

Let us explore David's responses to the Word of God, breaking down the responses for each of the view of the Word of God that he had. The analysis below is based on observing Psalm 119 on how David articulates his responses to each of the references that he speaks of, as you read you can do a similar exercise, discover other responses, and apply them to your life.

Learning from David's responses...

David a man after God's heart provides a great case study on how to respond to the word of God, which challenges our own relationship and engagement with the word of God. God deals with us differently; however, he gives us the opportunity to learn from the examples He has given us in His word and David is one of those amazing examples.

David stored up the word of God in his heart (Psalm 119:11). He took the word of God as a treasure to be hidden in his heart, keeping a reserve of the word in his heart. The bible teaches us that where your treasure is, your heart follows (Mathew 6:21), by storing the word in his heart he demonstrates what he values and what he allows to preoccupy his heart. Not only was his heart full of the word of God but his mind was also actively engaged as he shows that he was thinking of God's word and ways (Psalm 119: 52, 59), which would have allowed him to renew his mind (Romans 12:1-2). The way he engaged his heart and mind in his response to the word of God can be summed up by Colossians 3:16 " Let the word of Christ dwell in you richly, teaching and admonishing one another in all wisdom, singing psalms and hymns and spiritual songs, with thankfulness in your hearts to God". How can you start finding ways to have the word of God preoccupy your heart and mind?

The next response from David that I will deal with is quite interesting to me, which is he remembered the word of God and did not forget (Psalm 119:16, 61, 83, 87, 93, 109, 110, 141, 153, 176). The conversation between Jesus and his disciples changed my life regarding this response and portrays the depth of his response, in the book of John 14:25-26 Jesus comforted and taught his disciples as he prepared them for his death, resurrection and ascension. He came to a point He instructed them pertaining to the work of the Holy Spirit in their lives. The Holy Spirit would teach them all truth and remind them of the things that Jesus had taught them. The amazing part is that God teaches and reminds and in the same vein the expectation is for us to learn and remember. As we journey in our walk of faith we must learn and remember, the tendency is to want to seek new learning and not bring to remembrance the truth that we have already learnt to live and walk in it. Remembering enables believers to relate long enough with the truth, precepts, and commandments of God to live them out daily. The challenge to us then is whether we are relating long enough with the truth we know before seeking out for a new truth, the children of Israel were instructed to write the law of God on their door posts, gates, speak it to their children in the streets and in the houses (Deuteronomy 6:6-12) and also written in their hearts (Proverbs 7:3); and all was meant to help them to remember so they do not forget. In what ways are you nurturing the truth of God that you know, so you remember and not forget long enough to allow the truth to take root in your life and heart?

He responded by keeping the word of God (Psalm 119:17,57,67,101). He was quick to observe and perform what the word of God taught him (Psalm 119: 34, 112, 146). To him it was not enough to hear the word of God without corresponding performance of its dictates. This is observed further in this Psalm by some of his phrases that he uses to describe his responses; walk in God's rules(Psalm 119:1, 3), do God's commandments (Psalm 119: 166), and not swerve from your commandments (Psalm 119: 157). Naturally if something reveals a person's shortcomings or weakness they would want to run away and turn away but David was amazing he responded to the word by running in the way of God's commandments and turning his feet in the way of God's testimonies (Psalm 119:32, 59). The direction of his life travel, conduct, attitudes, and conversations were guided by the laws of God. There are a lot of elements to walking which are exciting to apply to our walk of faith and all those elements being guided by the laws of God is an amazing truth. David expanded this when he brings another aspect of walking for example your word is a lamp unto my feet and a light to my path (Psalm 119:105).He fixed his eyes on the commandments of God and setting the rules of God before his eyes (Psalm119:6, 30) he looked intently at the commandments of God, regarding them with pleasure, favour and care. Looking intently implies not allowing distractions to take away attention from God but to intentionally choose God's ways (Psalm 119:173). It takes courage and discipline, and the reason he was able to do this is because he considered the word of God to be right in all things (Psalm 119:128). Even his associations are linked to his response to the word of God as he indicates that his companionship was with those who keep His word (Psalm 119:63), for indeed bad company corrupts good character (1 Corinthians 15: 33). You can turn this into prayer points asking God to show you His available resources to help you have a passion to keep His word?

He put his trust in the word of God (Psalm 119:42). This shows that he found confidence and security in the word of God. Such an attitude would have given him boldness in his approach to life and tackling of the daily challenges that life threw at him. Trust is based on a relationship and this reveals that David was in an active relationship with God, clinging to His word (Psalm 119: 31). As a result of his trust in the word of God he put his hope in the word of God (Psalm 119: 43, 49,74,81,114,147). Hope is powerful in life, he responded to the word of God with expectation, which would have helped him with patience and perseverance when it came to him seeing God work in his life. Ultimately, he believed the word of God (Psalm 119:66), indeed faith comes by hearing and hearing by the word of God (Romans 10:17).

As a psalmist it is not surprising that he responded by singing (Psalm 119:172). What an expression of deep emotions of the heart through singing. Over the years I have come to realise the power of songs and the expression they give to life. David having had the word of God pre-occupy his life, he poured out his heart through singing, expressing his raw emotion when it came to relating with God and His word. Not only did he sing the songs, but he also made the songs (Psalm 119: 54) and paints an amazing picture of his worship by lifting his hands towards the word of God (Psalm 119:48); waking up at midnight to praise His word (Psalm 119: 62, 164,171).

The relationship of a student and a teacher can be seen emerge from how David responded to the word of God. He responded by learning the righteous rules of God (Psalm 119:7, 12, 71, 73). Learning consists of teaching, exercising in the taught subject and training; David's response was that of seeking to be taught of the righteous rules of God, exercising or practising the rules in order to grow and mature in them as well as seeking out practical training. This shows his response was an active response, I like the practising and training which reveals that our engagement with the word of God builds up overtime and we learn from our mistakes and acknowledge the grace of God through it all. The more we give ourselves to learning, the mature we become in our handling of the things of God. Being a keen learner of the rules of God, David responded by seeking to be taught the statutes by God himself (Psalm 119: 12, 26, 29, 33, 64, 68, 108, 124, 135, 171). He sought to be instructed and trained by the great teacher (God), receiving His counsel (Psalm 119: 24). It reveals David's heart, eagerness to learn and take instruction from God. It provides a glimpse into the level of communication that David and God had, two way rather than one directional. It challenges us believers to understand how God communicates with us and the primary way being His Word. Every day that God grants us it is an opportunity to be taught by Him as we see His rules, judgements, statutes, precepts, and commandments at work in our lives and around us.

Another response by David was to meditate on the precepts of God (Psalm 119: 15, 23, 48, 78, 97, 148). He pondered on God's communication which means he conversed with himself aloud or uttered; commune, complain, declare, muse, pray, speak, talk with himself and God. We will not be crazy when we find ourselves talking alone, pondering, and speaking aloud regarding a passage of scripture, I love it! Our meditation allows the word and revelation of God to deepen in our hearts and lives. He responded by declaring with his lips (Psalm 119:13). He spoke of the judgments (Psalm 119:46) of God recounting and celebrating them. He talked about them, his conversations were full of the judgments of God and what it meant for him and the nation of Israel. The depth of how he practised this is revealed when he highlights that his eyes are awake before dawn of night to meditate on God's promises (Psalm 119: 99). How can God help you overcome your fears and procrastination in developing this response?

What is also so evident and cannot be ignored is the strong affection and reverence he displayed towards the word, precepts, ways, commandments, and laws of God. He uses expressions that include delight (Psalm 119: 16, 35,47,70,77, 92, 143, 174); longing of the soul (Psalm 119:20, 40, 131); seek (Psalm 119:27, 34, 45, 73, 94), praise (Psalm 119: 164, 171), love (Psalm 119: 47, 48, 97, 113, 119, 127, 159, 163, 167). An amazing display of affection indeed, he rejoiced (Psalms 119: 111, 162) approaching the word of God with a display of joy, cheerfulness, and gladness. The way he explains it is like someone who has just found a great spoil, imagine such joy, and taking that as a response to the word of God. Additionally, his heart revered the word of God (Psalm 119: 120, 161). He did not take the word of God lightly but with awe and fear. The word of God teaches us that the fear of God is the beginning of all wisdom (Proverbs 9:10), he did not take it like mere words but as it is indeed the word of God (1 Thessalonians 2:13). How does this challenge your attitude and affection towards the word of God?

The response to the Word of God defines our level of engagement with God, and invariably our spiritual growth. David's responses reflect that it is intentional and deliberate, and the more we do it the more capacity we create for a deep fellowship with God through His word. How about a challenge to respond to the Word of God at a personal level, being sensitive to the opportunities God makes available to respond to His word and journal the impact in your life?

As I reflected on David's responses, I could see a pattern emerge so that we are not limited to David's experiences only. In fact, it liberates us and shows that it's a full-on relationship with the Word of God and not a set of activities we do. I saw truths emerge that can help us in our quest to respond to the Word of God. What was astounding was seeing the source of the response though they may have been expressed in different ways; effectively it was a response from his heart, soul, mind, all of his strength and with an overarching consciousness that it all started and ended with or in God. Jesus summarised this succinctly in Mark 12:30: "Love the Lord your God with all your heart, with all your soul, with all your mind, and with all your strength". David was convinced that it was not by his might or power, but by the Spirit of God that he was able to respond the way he did, regularly acknowledging and seeking God to teach or bring him understanding of His Word.

I encourage you to ask God to help you respond to His Word by your spirit, soul and body (heart, mind, soul, and all your strength) enabled by His Holy Spirit.

THE VALUE OF THE WORD OF GOD

The value and priority that David gives to the Word of God is apparent from his readiness to respond to the Word.

Our efforts and use of time are a full reflection of our heart's treasures and priorities.

David says, In the way of your testimonies I delight as much as in all riches (Psalms 119:14). He gave a comparison of the delight he would accord to all riches to that of the word of God. He further says, "the law of your mouth is better to me than thousands of gold and silver pieces" (Psalms 119:72), as if it was not enough, he adds that he loves God's commands above gold even the finest gold (Psalm 119:127). Even though he qualifies as one of the richest men ever to live in the world, yet he accords greater value to the Word of God.

David having been a man of war; understood the value of spoils obtained from enemies. Yet he says he rejoices at God's Word like one who finds great spoil (Psalms 119:162). We need to appreciate the level of riches that David had; gold, silver, kingdom, fame and all you name it! This gives a clear a picture of the value he placed on the Word of God above all else.

David pointed out something amazing, he says, "I have seen a limit to all perfection, but your commandment is exceedingly broad" (Psalms 119:96). How many times have we been in awe of technology, human achievements and discoveries? Yet David noted that the records are continually broken yet God's law is extremely broad and is without comparison and limitation. I remember listening to a sermon by Brother Robert Bayer titled The Incomparable Christ, in the sermon, he matched all the human legends and achievements yet Christ who is the final expression of God to humanity is incomparable.

Honey is sweet yet in David's value system; the word of God is sweeter than honey (Psalm 119:103).

David's son, Solomon in the book of proverbs highlights the greatness of wisdom and understanding (Proverbs 4:7) and David attributes the source of these to the Word of God. He says, your commandment makes me wiser than my enemies, for it is ever with me (Psalms 119:98). Additionally, the unfolding of your words gives light; it imparts understanding to the simple (Psalms 119:130).

Such is the regard that David had towards the Word of God, which explains the value and priority that he gave to the Word of God. It's easy to place high value on the material things and the riches of this world which we can see and touch, yet the Word of God which is spirit and life is of greater value (John 6:63). Paul puts it to us that we do not look at the things that are seen for they are temporal, but our focus should be on that which is not seen for they are eternal (2 Corinthians 4:18). The Word of God is eternal and of great value. The value of something is dependent upon its usefulness and ability to bring transformation, change to an individual, circumstance, or a need(s). David's conviction therefore is that the Word of God is more useful and has the ability to bring transformation or change to an individual, circumstance, or a need(s) more than riches or anything else in this world.

GOD'S PART OR FACTOR IN RELATING WITH HIS WORD

After considering how David viewed and responded to the Word of God, we run the risk of getting into a performance mode thinking that it is just a formula of getting the most out of the Word and arm twist God so to say. We need to hasten to acknowledge the God factor when it comes to the operation of His Word.

Paul noted this in the letter to the Corinthians, he planted, and Apollos watered, but *God gave the growth* (1 Corinthians 3:6).

In his relationship with the Word, David equally acknowledges the part that God plays, and this is well summed up by prophet Jeremiah when God points out that He watches over His Word to perform it (Jeremiah 1:12). Therefore, as David engages with the Word, God is using every opportunity to perform His Word in David's life. This creates a heart of a reverential relationship with the Word as we realise, we are relating with the person of God as they are inseparable.

Below is an outline of some of the ways that David acknowledges God's involvement with His Word:

1. He is the teacher of His Word (Psalm 119 vs 171, 135, 124, 108, 102, 66, 33, 29, 26, 12).
2. He gives life according to His Word (Psalm 119 vs 159, 156, 154, 149, 107, 93, 50, 25).
3. He is the giver of understanding according to His Word (Psalm 119 vs 169, 144, 125, 73, 34, 27).
4. His Word hinges on His righteousness and faithfulness (Psalm 119 vs 138, 137, 90, 89, 75).

5. He is our lover (Psalm 119 vs 88, 76, 64, 41).
6. He is the helper and comforter according to His Word (Psalm 119 vs 86, 82, 76, 50).
7. He gives honour and turns away reproach (Psalm 119 vs 39, 31, 22, 21).
8. He delivers according to His Word (Psalm 119 vs 170, 153, 110).
9. God hears and answers (Psalm 119 vs 145, 149, 26).
10. He saves according to His Word (Psalm 119 vs 94, 81, 41).
11. He is the revealer of truths (Psalm 119 vs 18, 19).
12. He keeps our feet steady according to His Word (Psalm 119 vs 133, 117).
13. God acts in according to people's response to His Word (Psalm 119 vs 126, 118).
14. He is good and does good (Psalm 119 vs 68, 65).
15. He gives favour and grace (Psalm 119 vs 58, 29).
16. He leads us in His path (Psalm 119 vs 35, 10.
17. He is the source of His Word (Psalm 119 vs 152).
18. He breaks the dominion of iniquity over us according to His Word (Psalm 119 vs 133).
19. God fulfils His Word (Psalm 119 vs 123).
20. He upholds us according to his Word (Psalm 119 vs 116).
21. He receives praise (Psalm 119 vs 10).
22. He is the Judge (Psalm 119 vs 84).
23. He is merciful (Psalm 119 vs 77).
24. He is our maker (Psalm 119 vs 73).
25. He is our portion (Psalm 119 vs 57).
26. He turns our eyes from looking at worthless things (Psalm 119 vs 37).
27. He inclines our hearts to His Word (Psalm 119 vs 36).
28. He enlarges our hearts (Psalm 119 vs 32).
29. He is the giver of strength (Psalm 119 vs 28).

Some years back, I was stirred in my heart by David's words in (Psalms 78:41 NKJV); when he said that the children of Israel limited the Holy One of Israel. Imagine the omnipotent, omnipresent, omniscient God; being limited by human beings or believers. Yet as believers, we can limit the operation of God in our lives if we do not create the capacity by giving Him the material to work with, which is His Word in us, which he watches over to perform.

The gospels record that as the disciples went about preaching, he was with them confirming His Word with signs and wonders. Do you see what he was confirming, His word! (Mark 16:20).

Joshua was told to meditate on God's Word day and night and by so doing he will make his way prosperous, this is because of the God factor, God watching over His Word in Joshua to perform it (Joshua1:8). We need to have this mindset as we approach the Word of God; the acknowledgement of the God factor humbles us and overflows into worship.

THE IMPACT OF GOD'S WORD IN THE BELIEVER'S LIFE

The opening verses to Psalm 119 sum up the impact of responding to the Word of God as being 'blessed', that is empowered to live a victorious life in Christ (Psalm 119:1–2).

By observing David's comments, we can see how this manifested in his life.

1. Provides ability to walk in the ways of God (*Psalm 119* vs 3).
2. Receives honour instead of shame and reproach (*Psalm 119* vs 6, 22).
3. Offers God genuine praise from an upright heart (*Psalm 119* vs 7, 164,171).
4. Enjoys the consciousness of the presence of God daily (*Psalm 119* vs 8).
5. The Purity of ways (*Psalm 119* vs 9).
6. Pursues God, His Kingdom and His righteousness (*Psalm 119* vs 10).
7. Dominion over sin (*Psalm 119* vs 11, 101).
8. Privy to the wondrous things in God's word (*Psalm 119* vs18).
9. Chose the way of faithfulness (*Psalm 119* vs 30).
10. Received comfort in affliction (*Psalm 119* vs 50, 52).
11. Inheritance in God (*Psalm 119* vs 57).
12. Became a testimony of the goodness of God (*Psalm 119* vs 74).
13. Received life –God's kind of life (*Psalm 119* vs 93).
14. Received great wisdom (*Psalm 119* vs 98).
15. Received great understanding (Psalm 119 vs 99, 100, 104, 130).

16. Illumination and true light (*Psalm 119* vs 105, 130).
17. Found a hiding place and shield in God (*Psalm 119* vs 114).
18. Zeal for the things of God (*Psalm 119* vs 139).
19. An all-encompassing relationship with God.
20. Advocate in God (*Psalm 119* vs 154).
21. Salvation (*Psalm 119* vs 155).
22. He found the truth (*Psalm 119* vs 160).
23. Great peace (*Psalm 119* vs 165).

Indeed, the result for David was a victorious life of a real person, with real life issues and real faith. What a challenge to our faith and relationship with God.

As I wrote these reflections, I had a life-transforming realization. What makes any natural relationship great is the moments shared? It is the moments we share with God, which make us ordinary people extraordinary. We share these moments through engagement with His Word, prayer and fellowship with His Spirit.

Paul in his parting words to the Corinthians says, may the fellowship (Greek – koinonia) of the Holy Spirit be with you (2 Corinthians 13:14). This is our calling, fellowship with the Father and His son Jesus Christ; and one way of doing this is engaging with His Word (1 John 1:1–4).

4.

WORD FITNESS FOR NEW BELIEVERS

... as new-born babes, desire the pure milk of the word...

In my early years as a believer, I received encouragement to read the Bible (Word). What to do (read) was clear but how to read was not clear. It is easier to encourage what to read without the how part. In 2010, I attended a course on how to read the Bible, and after finishing the course I questioned myself why the teaching of these basics was not common in churches. An important take away for me was the attitude towards studying or reading the Bible. Approaching the Word with this attitude has changed my reading. The first attitude is that of observing what is in the text, secondly getting meaning out of the text and finally applying the meaning of the text to my life. I remember the lecturer emphasising that we need to spend more time observing the text before rushing to try to get the meaning. I felt a weight lift after realising I should not be under pressure to rush to get what the text means, but rather the more I observe the ease for God to use the text to speak to me. Then the challenge is on applying the Word, it is not enough to just observe or interpret without applying the Word to our lives.

Observation of the text

What do I see? What are the facts? Psalms 119:18. In psalms 119, David highlights a few pointers about his reading that we can employ.

a. Pray when you read and after reading the texts.
b. Read out of the text and not into the text, which is not to bring preconceived ideas to the text you are reading.
c. See the text from the perspectives of all the characters.
d. Question the text using the basic questions of who, what, when, where, why and how.
e. Meditate on the text, which is to replay the text to yourself in your mind and speaking to yourself.
f. Apply your imagination to the text to see the emotion, atmosphere and character of the text.
g. Read the text more than once.
h. Read the text out aloud to yourself.
i. Sing the text out to yourself.
j. Share with other believers what you are seeing.

Interpretation of the text

What does it mean? Quest for meaning/understanding (Psalms 119:34, Acts 8:26-30).

The meaning of the text is the overarching truth that God is conveying out of the text. The initial attitude is to understand what it meant to the original audience before imposing the meaning to your current circumstances. The truth of God is not limited to time, culture, tradition, era, or language. Secondly, there is need for the separation of the truth from the elements bound by the limitations noted above.

Thirdly, you need to consider what the coming of Jesus has accomplished. Lastly identify the truth that God is communicating to you considering the work that Christ did for you. It is then imperative to devote enough time in observing, to create capacity for accurate interpretation.

Application of the text

How does it work in my life? How does it work in others' lives (Transformed lives and communities) (Titus 1:1, Romans 12:2)?

The ultimate purpose of the word is to bring change in our personal lives, communities and the world around us. We must learn to be honest with ourselves to accept the teaching, correction, rebuke and training of the Word of God (2 Timothy 3:16). With humility, we then take the Word and start to practice it in the direction of the truth revealed. Allow the Word of God to do the work in you, opening up more and staying the course. Paul says the message of the cross is foolishness to those that are perishing but the power of God to those being saved (1 Corinthians 1:18).

We can help fellow new believers in their faith journey by teaching them how to read the Bible. This is an amazing journey to knowing God and His full revelation. Jesus said this is eternal life that they know you the true God (John 17:3).

5.

WHAT NEXT? – WORD FITNESS!

The book of Hebrews helps us to understand that the Word of God is living and active (Hebrews 4:12-13), this is important in shifting our mindset towards how we relate with the Word of God. If you are not careful, you may end up being consumed in getting the scriptures into your head or memory, but that should be the means and not the end. The Word being alive and active cannot be confined to a human memory or brain.

Further in Hebrews 4:2, we are told the Word they received did not profit them for they did not mix it with faith. We have to respond to the Word of God in faith, the Bible makes it clear that without faith it is impossible to please God for when we come to Him we must believe that he exists and that he rewards those who diligently seek Him (Hebrews 11:6). Anytime we discuss faith, we need to get it clear in our minds that the critical elements to faith are the object of our faith (God), the source of our faith (His Word) and the response of our faith (works of faith). The hearing of the Word of God is the source of faith, this means that we have to recognise and acknowledge the authority of the Word, the Word of God is infallible, and it is without error. The reason for this is that it was inspired by God (2 Timothy 3:16) and it is our expression of faith when we take Him at His Word. The historicity of the Word of God amazes me, this can be proved from books other than the Bible and I do not say this as if I need that to believe but to buttress the fact that our faith is not a blind faith.

We believe in God who has chosen to express Himself to us by inspiring our forerunners and now we have the legacy of the oracles of the most High God, which is the Bible.

Imagine this, if the Word is the sword of the Spirit then a complete picture has to be to have the soldier and his sword (Ephesians 6:17). The full efficacy of the Word has to come from a full relationship with both the Word and the Holy Spirit. Apostle Paul in his farewell words in a letter to the Corinthians intimates, the grace of our Lord Jesus, the love of the Father and fellowship of the Holy Spirit be with you all (2 Corinthians 13:14). We are called to fellowship, this is not a passive process, and neither is it one sided but rather multifaceted.

I talk about a relationship with the Word of God a lot, but just to say a relationship on its own is not enough to express that which I intent to communicate. Naturally, a relationship simply refers to the nature of connection between parties or people. I am not talking about just being an acquaintance, colleague, workmate, church member with the Word of God; oh no, it is much deeper than that. The onus is on yourself to evaluate your current relationship with the Word of God and where you desire it to be. Let us break this down, in 1 John 1:1-4, the Apostle testifies of hearing, seeing, and handling the Word of life that was from the beginning. He further says the intention of their testifying was so that we may join them in fellowship, of which that fellowship is with the Father and the Son, Jesus the Christ.

Therefore, the call to us is fellowship with the Father and with His Son, Jesus. I then say to myself, of course John, you had the privilege of hearing by the scriptures of old being the Law of Moses, Prophets and Psalms (Luke 24:44) and actually walking with Jesus that is why you can say such things with conviction.

I can almost hear him say to me, come on brother, have you not read and understood what I said in my earlier writing (John 14:15-31)? I know Jesus was with us, but before He was taken up he clearly promised that He will not leave believers alone. He sent someone of the same kind as He was, that is the Holy Spirit. He would further say to me, I understand your concern that you cannot see, hear or touch Him, but He addressed that as well. Jesus said that when the Holy Spirit comes the world will not see or recognise but the believers will know Him, not only will He be with us but also in us.

At this point I would be intently listening to John explaining; brother, by the Holy Spirit being with and in us, Jesus said it would be Himself and the Father dwelling in us. We had fellowship with Jesus, and our fellowship was with the Word of life and now you have fellowship with the Holy Spirit, like brother Paul said in his letter to the Corinthians. The world may not recognise Him, but you have the written word as the mirror into this spirit-filled life (James 1:23-25). For you to relate with the word you have to relate with the Holy Spirit and vice versa. I would then conclude the conversation by saying, thanks John I now understand that relating with the word is an intentional full-on fellowship with the word and the Holy Spirit.

When talking of relating with God, there are intriguing matters that come to mind. It is possible to relate to the history and reputation of God without relating to the person of God. Jesus is asked by His disciples to show them the Father and his response was, have you not been with me long enough to know that I am in the Father and the Father is in me. He further says believe in me or else for the works that I do (John 14:11–12).

The disciples related with the person of God through fellowship with Jesus, John makes this clear in I John 1:1–4. Likewise, when He was about to go back to heaven, He promised that He would not leave us alone but would send another person of the same kind as Him, the Holy Spirit, to be with and in us. We therefore fellowship with the person of God through the fellowship with Holy Spirit, which explains Paul's concluding remarks in his letter to the Corinthian church, "and the fellowship of the Holy Spirit be with you" (2 Corinthians 13:14).

So mightily grew the Word of God...

"So, the Word of the Lord continued to increase and prevail," Acts 19:20. Be encouraged the Word of God will grow and prevail over all areas of your life as you connect intimately with God through His Word (The Bible). In case you have read this book, but you are not a believer, Jesus loves and is ready to save you. What shall you do then to be saved? Well a similar question was asked in Acts 16:30–31, believe in the Lord!

WORD FITNESS WORKBOOK

Just as in physical exercises, one has to practice in order to attain certain levels of fitness. Below are a few 'word fitness' exercises to help you reflect and put into practice some of the truths discussed in the various chapters. Word fitness is critical to a victorious Christian life. You can use these exercises as individuals or as groups as you dive into the Word of God.

The purpose of the Word of God – Personal reflections

1. What has God impressed on your heart in this chapter and how are you going to respond?

    a. Do you know yourself?
    b. You can have a changed life.
    c. The Word of God has power to transform lives
    d. What does a transformed life look like?

2. What have you learnt about God?
3. Read Psalms 119: 1–26:

    a. Read silently.
    b. Read out aloud to yourself.
    c. Find prayer points from the verses.

Nurturing the relationship with the word of God – Personal reflections

1. What has God impressed on your heart in this chapter and how are you going to respond?

    a. David's view of the word of God.
    b. David's response to the word of God.
    c. The value of the word of God to David.
    d. God's part or factor in relation to His Word.
    e. The impact of God's Word on David's life.

2. What have you learnt about God?
3. What does being in a relationship with the word of God mean to you?
4. Read Psalms 119: 27–64:

    a. Read silently.
    b. Read out aloud to yourself.
    c. Find prayer points from the verses.
    d. Find verses that address areas highlighted in reflection question 1.

The nature of the Word of God – Personal reflections

1. What has God impressed on your heart in this chapter and how are you going to respond?

    a. The words I have spoken to you are spirit and life.
    b. The written Word of God.
    c. Jesus Christ the Word of God.
    d. The Word of God being alive and active.

e. The Word of God as an incorruptible seed.
  f. New Testament references to the Word of God.

2. What have you learnt about God?
3. What change will knowing the nature of the word of God bring to your life?
4. Read Psalms 119: 65–104:

   a. Read silently.
   b. Read out aloud to yourself.
   c. Find prayer points from the verses.

Word fitness for new believers – Personal reflections

1. What has God impressed on your heart in this chapter and how are you going to respond?

   a. Observation of the text.
   b. Interpretation of the text.
   c. Application of the text.

2. What have you learnt about God?
3. How are you going to read the Bible differently?
4. Read Psalms 119: 105–176 and practice the Bible study for beginners' guides:

   a. Observation.
   b. Interpretation.
   c. Application

5. How are you going to help other believers to read the Bible?

Personal transformed life exercise

Practice identifying the truths in God's word that show your true identity in Christ Jesus. See how they affect your life and thank God for the truths. Example below from Paul's letter.

Ephesians 4:17-31 comparison of the old self and new self – manner of life (the believer's daily transformation).

Old self	New self	Transformation Overarching application
Thief.	No longer steal, labour, doing honest work with his own hands, so that he may have something to share with anyone in need.	Work ethic and renewed purpose for the fruit of our labour.
Put away falsehood.	Speak the truth with his neighbour.	Healthy conversations and relationships.
		Decision making influence.
Grieve the Holy Spirit	Do not grieve the Holy Spirit of God,	Relationship with God and the Holy Spirit.
		Attitude and condition of heart.
… bitterness, wrath, anger, clamour, slander, and malice.	Be kind to one another, tender-hearted, forgiving one another, as God in Christ forgave you.	Motives/desires.

Old self	New self	Transformation Overarching application
No hope.	… the Holy Spirit of God, by whom you were sealed for the day of redemption.	Hope of destiny.
Be angry and sin; let the sun go down on your anger and give opportunity to the devil.	Be angry and do not sin; do not let the sun go down on your anger and give no opportunity to the devil.	Respond to world's challenges or temptations and the ultimate impact.
Corrupting talk come out of your mouths.	Let no corrupting talk come out of your mouths, but only such as is good for building up, as fits the occasion, that it may give grace to those who hear.	Wise use of words realising their power of life and death.

Responding to the Word of God as...

Below is a summary of how David responded to the Word of God. Can you think of how this applies to your life and how you are growing in your response to His Word? You can write your thoughts at the bottom.

The Truth and Word

1. Stored up in the heart (Psalm 119 vs 11).
2. Remember (not forget) (Psalm 119 vs16).
3. Keep (Psalm 119 vs 17, 57, 67, 101).
4. Trust in the Word (Psalm 119 vs 42)
5. Hope in your word (Psalm 119 vs 49, 74, 81, 114, 147).
6. Heart reveres your words (Psalm 119 vs 161).
7. Rejoice (Psalm 119 vs 162).
8. Tongue will sing of your words (Psalm 119 vs 172).

The Rules/ Precepts /Commandments/Law

1. Declared with lips (Psalm 119 vs 13).
2. Keep (with whole heart) (Psalm 119 vs 4, 5, 8, 33, 34, 44, 55, 56, 60, 63, 69, 100, 106, 115, 134, 145, 168).
3. Walk in (Psalm 119 vs 1).
4. Fix eyes on (Psalm 119 vs 6).
5. Learn righteous rules (Psalm 119 vs 7, 12, 71, 73).
6. Seek to be taught by God (Psalm 119 vs 12, 26, 29, 33, 64, 68, 108, 124, 135, 171).
7. Meditate (Psalm 119 vs 15, 23, 48, 78, 97, 148.)
8. Delight (Psalm 119 vs 16, 35, 47, 70, 77, 92, 143, 174).
9. Seek the Lord to open eyes to see the wondrous things in His law (Psalm 119 vs 19).

10. Longing of the soul (Psalm 119 vs 20, 40, 131).
11. Seek the Lord to understand (Psalm 119 vs 27, 34, 73).
12. Set the Lord's rules before (Psalm 119 vs 30).
13. Run in the way of your commandments (Psalm 119 vs 32).
14. Observe with whole heart (Psalm 119 vs 34).
15. Hope in your rules (Psalm 119 vs 43).
16. Seek your precepts (Psalm 119 vs 45, 94).
17. Love (Psalm 119 vs 47, 48, 97, 113, 127, 159, 163).
18. Lift hands towards (Psalm 119 vs 48).
19. Think of (Psalm 119 vs 52).
20. Make songs (Psalm 119 vs 54).
21. Remember (not forget/ forsake) (Psalm 119 vs 61,83, 87, 93, 109, 110, 141, 153, 176).
22. At midnight arise and praise (Psalm 119 vs 62).
23. Companion of those who keep (Psalm 119 vs 63).
24. Believe (Psalm 119 vs 66).
25. Perform your statutes (Psalm 119 vs 112).
26. Have regard for your statutes (Psalm 119 vs 117).
27. Afraid of your judgements (Psalm 119 vs 120).
28. Praise the Lord because of His righteous rules (Psalm 119 vs 164, 171).
29. I do your commandments (Psalm 119 vs 166).
30. Choose your precepts (Psalm 119 vs 173).
31. Consider all to be right (Psalm 119 vs 128).

The Testimonies

1. Delight (Psalm 119 vs 14, 24).
2. Keep (Psalm 119 vs 2, 22, 88, 129, 167, 168).
3. Receive counsel (Psalm 119 vs 24).
4. Cling to (Psalm 119 vs 31).

5. Speak of (Psalm 119 vs 46).
6. Turn feet to your testimonies (Psalm 119 vs 59).
7. Know your testimonies (Psalm 119 vs 125).
8. Consider your testimonies (Psalm 119 vs 95).
9. The joy of heart (Psalm 119 vs 111).
10. Eyes awake before dawn of night to meditate on your promise (Psalm 119 vs 99).
11. Not swerve from your testimonies (Psalm 119 vs 157).
12. I love (Psalm 119 vs 119, 167).
13. Observe (Psalm 119 vs 146).

His ways

1. Walk in (Psalm 119 vs 3).
2. Fix eyes (Psalm 119 vs 15).
3. Think on your ways (Psalm 119 vs 59).

ACKNOWLEDGMENTS

With great appreciation to my wife Caroline, my dad and mum Wilbert and Janet Maponda and my dear brothers and sisters in Christ who have helped me in my walk with God. Thank you for your great help in putting together that which God laid on my heart in this book.

Thanks be to the All Wise God; the grace of my Lord Jesus Christ, the love of the Father and the fellowship of the Holy Spirit for the amazing truths laid on my heart and in my life pertaining the words of life which come from God.

Lightning Source UK Ltd.
Milton Keynes UK
UKHW041335231221
396076UK00010B/173